P9-ELG-321

CH

MAY   2014

DISCARD
Westminster Public Library
3705 W. 112th Ave.
Westminster, CO 80031
www.westminsterlibrary.org

Discovery
EDUCATION™

Published in 2014 by The Rosen Publishing Group, Inc.
29 East 21st Street, New York, NY 10010

Copyright © 2014 Weldon Owen Pty Ltd. Originally published in 2011 by Discovery Communications, LLC

Original copyright © 2011 Discovery Communications, LLC. Discovery Education™ and the Discovery Education logo are trademarks of Discovery Communications, LLC, used under license. All rights reserved.

All rights reserved. No part of this book may be reproduced in any form without permission in writing from the publisher, except by a reviewer.

Photo Credits: Key t=top; l=left; r=right; tl=top left; tc=top center; tcr=top center right; tr=top right; cl=center left; c=center; cr=center right; b=bottom; bl=bottom left; bc=bottom center; br=bottom right; bg=background

CBT = Corbis; DT = Dreamstime; iS = istockphoto.com; OS = ourswaps.com; SH = Shutterstock; TF = Topfoto; TPL = photolibrary.com; wiki = Wikipedia

front cover iS; **4**bc, c iS; br TF; **4–5**bc, bg iS; tc SH; **5**bl iS; **6**tl, tr, bg iS; **7**br, cl, tr, bg iS; **8**bl CBT; br OS; **8–9**bg TPL; **10**bl, br, cr, bg iS; **11** bl, bl, bl, br, br, c, tl, tl, tl, tr, tr, bg iS; **12**b iS; tr TF; **12–13**bg iS; **13**bc, c iS; cr, tc, SH; cl TF; **14**bc, bl, br iS; br SH; bl TPL; bc wiki; **14–15**bg CBT; **15**bc, bl, br iS; bc, bl, br SH; **16**bl, cr, l, l, tl iS; **16–17**bg iS; **17**bc, tl, tr iS; tl SH; **20**cl DT; bl iS; **20–21**bc iS; **21**br DT; tr SH; **22**tr CBT; c, c iS; bl, br TF; **23**bl CBT; r, r iS; cr, tl TF; **24**tc, cr, bg iS; bc SH; **25**br, cl, bg iS; **26**tl, br TF; bl, tr TPL; **27**cr iS; bl, c, tl, tr TF; **28**b, bl SH; **28–29**bg iS; tc SH; **29**br CBT; **30**bg iS; **31**bl, bl, cl, tcr, cr, tl, tr, tr, bg iS; br SH; **32**bg iS

All illustrations copyright Weldon Owen Pty Ltd

Weldon Owen Pty Ltd
Managing Director: Kay Scarlett
Creative Director: Sue Burk
Publisher: Helen Bateman
Senior Vice President, International Sales: Stuart Laurence
Vice President Sales North America: Ellen Towell
Administration Manager, International Sales: Kristine Ravn

Library of Congress Cataloging-in-Publication Data

Brasch, Nicolas.
 The invention of money / by Nicolas Brasch.
    p. cm. — (Discovery education : discoveries and inventions)
 Includes index.
 ISBN 978-1-4777-1333-4 (library binding) — ISBN 978-1-4777-1508-6 (pbk.) —
ISBN 978-1-4777-1509-3 (6-pack)
 1. Money—History—Juvenile literature. I. Title.
 HG221.5.B73 2014
 332.4'9—dc23

                    2012043621

Manufactured in the United States of America

CPSIA Compliance Information: Batch #S13PK3: For Further Information contact Rosen Publishing, New York, New York at 1-800-237-9932

DISCOVERIES AND INVENTIONS

THE INVENTION OF MONEY

NICOLAS BRASCH

PowerKiDS press

New York

Contents

Why We Need Money

Before there was money, people swapped items to get what they wanted. However, this system was far from perfect, and money was invented to make life easier for both buyers and sellers. One reason why we still use money is that it is far more convenient to carry around bills and coins than it is to carry around objects we may want to swap. It is also convenient because everyone has a need for it. Before there was money, someone who had an object to swap needed to find someone who wanted that object.

Another reason why we use money is that money has a certain value that everyone agrees to. No one can argue how much a dollar or a euro is worth. If there was no money, buyers and sellers would argue over the value of the items they were swapping.

Small change
People carry coins to pay for everyday items such as newspapers or parking meters.

> *Money alone sets all
> the world in motion.*
>
> **PUBLILIUS SYRUS,
> ROMAN WRITER AND POET, 100 BC**

Works of art
Some bills are almost works of art.
This German 100-mark bill from 1908
shows remarkable detail on both sides.
Bills also offer governments the
opportunity to display aspects of
their country's history and values.

Revolving roles
A shopkeeper sells an item
to someone and then uses the
money she receives to buy an
item for herself. The shopkeeper
she pays will then go on to spend
some of that money buying an item
from someone else. Buyers become
sellers, sellers become buyers,
and this is how money circulates.

Bartering

The system of swapping goods or services, rather than using money, is called bartering. Bartering was used before money was invented. It is still used today in some places. In fact, bartering is very common in school playgrounds. Some children swap cards in the playground, which is a form of bartering. Not all cards are the same value. If someone wants a particular card, they may offer two or more cards as a swap.

Ideally, bartering involves two people directly swapping goods or services. In ancient times, this may have involved animals, such as swapping two sheep for a cow. The problem with bartering is that it often involves several transactions because the person with two sheep may not want a cow. They may actually want a rug. Then again, someone with a spare rug may need a water jug. Such complications are the main reason that money has replaced bartering.

That's Amazing!

European expansion between 1500 and 1800 was built on bartering. Goods wanted in Asia, Africa, the Americas, and the Pacific were sent by ship and swapped for spices, plants, and valuable minerals.

Online bartering

Today, bartering groups use the Internet to link buyers and sellers. Internet traders offer goods, such as furniture or children's toys, and services, such as legal work or home decoration.

Worthless money
After World War I, the German economy was in such a poor state that money had become almost worthless. So people swapped goods, rather than using money.

Barter market
This market in Mali in Africa, uses
bartering rather than money
to buy and sell goods.

Coins

The first coins were invented about 2,500 years ago in Lydia, Asia Minor, and China. They were made out of precious metals such as gold, silver, and bronze. The value of these early coins was determined by weight. The heavier they were, the more valuable they were. To make it easy for people to figure out the worth of coins, their value was indicated by a stamp on each one. The process of stamping is known as minting.

One problem with using valuable minerals to make coins was that it became harder to find such minerals. Also, some people began shaving the edges of coins, melting this waste down, and then reselling the valuable mineral. As a result, governments began to make coins out of less valuable minerals and stamp them with a value. This is still done today with the coins we use.

Fact or Fiction?

The kingdom of Lydia no longer exists, but its area is now part of Turkey. According to the Greek historian Herodotus, Lydians were the first people to use gold and silver coins.

Ancient Chinese coins
The first Chinese coins were made out of bronze. Some of them even had holes in the middle so they could be tied to a piece of string and kept together.

Doubloons
Doubloons were gold coins used by Spain until the mid-1800s. They were made from gold mined in South America and shipped back to Spain. Because of their value, they were greatly sought-after by pirates.

United States of America
Coins from the United States date back to the late 1800s and include the buffalo nickel and the Indian penny.

Japan
The Japanese unit of currency is the yen. Coins come as 1, 5, 10, 50, 100, and 500 yen. The 5-yen coin and the silver 50-yen coin, shown above, have holes in them.

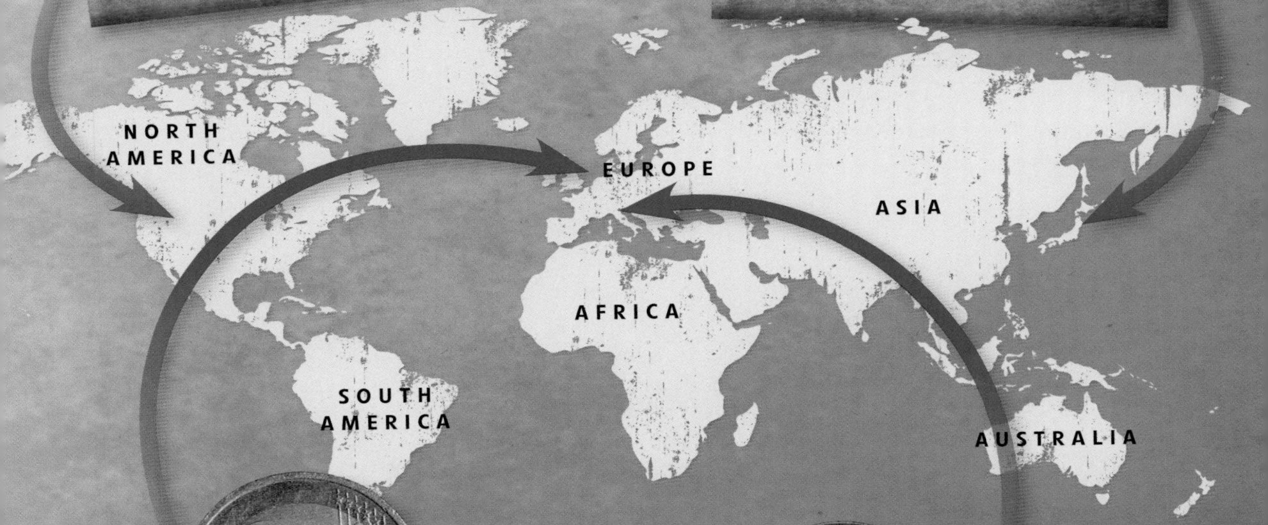

NORTH AMERICA

EUROPE

ASIA

AFRICA

SOUTH AMERICA

AUSTRALIA

Euro
The euro has been the currency of many European nations since 1999. One side shows a map of Europe and the reverse depends on the country issuing it. The reverse of this 2-euro coin shows the German coat of arms.

Vatican City
Even the smallest country in the world, Vatican City, has its own coins. These are 100-Vatican City lira, though Vatican City now calls its coins euros.

Paper Money

The first banknotes were produced by the Chinese more than 1,000 years ago. They saw that bills had two main advantages over metal coins. One advantage was that they were lighter to carry. Someone needing to make a large purchase previously had to carry a heavy load of coins. Also, while the valuable minerals used to make some coins were becoming scarce, paper was cheap and plentiful. Paper bills proved to be the solution.

The use of bills took several hundred years to spread from China to Europe. The first European banknotes were pieces of paper that promised the transfer of a certain amount of gold or silver from the buyer to the seller.

Norwegian banknote
This 1695 Norwegian banknote is one of Europe's oldest existing banknotes.

Chinese banknote
One side of this Chinese 5-jiao bill has an image of two children. The other side shows the Chinese coat of arms.

Malaysian banknote
Malaysia started producing its own bills in 1967. This is the 100-dollar bill. In 1975, "ringgit" replaced the term "dollar."

Eritrean banknote
This 1-nakfa bill from Eritrea shows three children who attend a rural school.

Egyptian banknote
The Egyptian 50-piastres bill features an image of the statue of Ramses II in front of a sun boat and some lotus flowers.

Russian banknote
These 5-ruble bills from Russia were produced in 1909 and have an amazing amount of detail.

That's Amazing!
The largest banknote in the world is the 100,000-piso bill issued by the government of the Philippines in 1998. The bill measures 14 inches by 8½ inches (355.6 mm by 215.9 mm).

Euro banknotes
The euro is the second most-traded currency in the world, after the US dollar.

Precious Objects

Before coins and banknotes were invented, communities used precious objects as a form of currency. The type of object they used depended on what was available and how rare it was. For example, communities that lived near a coast often used beautiful seashells. Many communities used metals and minerals that they could dig up from the ground. Some communities used rare parts of animals, such as ivory from elephants. Trading precious objects instead of coins and banknotes is still practiced in many communities today.

Cowrie shells
These shells have most commonly been traded through Africa and Asia. Their smooth, shiny surface is pleasing to look at, and their hardness means they are longlasting and can be traded many times.

Wampum beads
Quahog shells were used to make wampum beads by Native Americans. But it was the Europeans, not Native Americans, who used them as currency in the mid-to-late 1600s.

Manila rings
Originally made for use as currency among African communities, Europeans started using manila rings to buy and sell African slaves. One manila ring equaled one human.

Tea bricks
Tea bricks are compressed tea leaves formed in the shape of bricks. In ancient China, tea bricks were used as a way of storing tea leaves, as well as a form of currency.

Tobacco
In colonial times, tobacco was used as currency in several American colonies, such as Virginia, North Carolina, and Maryland. It was grown as a crop to be sold, not consumed.

Ivory
The rarer an item, the more its value as currency. Ivory from the tusks of elephants is very rare, and has long been used as currency in Africa to trade for other goods.

Gold ingots
In times of war, economic depression, and other major events, many people buy gold to protect their wealth if the value of their country's currency falls dramatically.

Banking

Banks are businesses that buy and sell money. They buy money from people or businesses that have money to spare. They then sell this money to other people or businesses that need large amounts of money to buy something else. The main way that banks make their profit is by selling money for a price that is higher than the price for which they bought it.

Depositing money

People deposit money into a bank when they do not need it for a certain period of time. Depositing money in a bank is safer than keeping it at home. Also, people receive interest (extra money paid by the bank) on the money they deposit.

ATMs

ATM stands for automated teller machine. These machines are located outside banks or other buildings and enable people to make withdrawals or deposits at any time. Before ATMs, people could only deposit and withdraw money during a bank's business hours.

Banking online

The Internet has made it much easier for people to make transactions to and from their bank account. Before the Internet, people wanting to make transactions had to visit a bank branch and submit forms. Today, people can do much of their banking without leaving home.

Direct debit

This is a way of transferring money electronically from the bank account of a purchaser into the bank account of the business or person selling goods or services. The use of direct debit means that people do not have to carry around a lot of cash.

Borrowing money

Businesses or individuals often borrow money for something they could not otherwise afford, such as a house or new equipment for a factory. Eventually, they have to pay back this money, as well as an extra amount known as interest.

Financial advice

Banks also give financial advice. Financial advisers take into account the amount of money a person has, how old the person is, how much the person needs for everyday use, and other circumstances.

Creating Interest

nterest is the amount of money that a bank pays out to people who deposit money with the bank. It is also the amount of money the bank receives from people who borrow money from it.

This sequence of illustrations shows how interest is calculated and how it keeps banks in business. Although the illustrations show actual money being handled, most transactions today are done electronically.

2. Bank stores money in vault
The money from the depositor is put into a vault for safekeeping.

1. Customer deposits money into bank
This depositor will receive 5 percent interest each year for the money he has deposited. For example, if he deposits 1,000 dollars, he will receive 50 dollars after every 12 months that the money is in the bank.

3. Bank lends to borrower
The bank manager explains to the customers they must pay 10 percent each year in interest for the money they want to borrow. They also have to pay back the borrowed amount over an agreed period of time.

4. Bank draws money out of vault
The bank manager takes money out of the bank vault and hands it to the borrower.

5. Making a profit
A bank makes a profit by lending out the money it borrows from people.

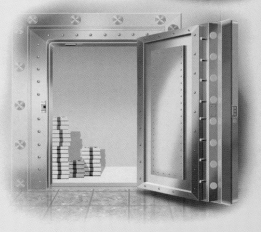

Staying in business
If a bank lends out all or most of the money that it has borrowed from people, then it will make a profit. This is because it is receiving more in interest from the people they lent it to than it has to pay to the people they borrowed the money from.

Out of business
If a bank cannot lend the money that it has borrowed from people, then it will soon go out of business. It will have to pay out more in interest than it receives in interest.

?... You Decide

I s credit a good or a bad thing? Credit is the borrowing of money to buy something now, with the promise of paying back the borrowed amount over an agreed period of time, with interest. Credit can be obtained through an agreement with a bank, or by the use of a credit card.

Pros of credit
The main pros of using credit are the ability to buy something expensive without having to save up first, and the flexibility of buying online or by phone.

Traveling on vacation
Many tourists pay for goods and services with a credit card to save them from carrying around a lot of cash. They can also buy more than they can afford and pay the extra amount back over time, when they return home.

Buying a house
Saving up to buy a house would take most people many years. Buying a house on credit means they can live in the house while paying it off.

Shopping online
Credit cards are ideal for making purchases over the Internet. Internet shopping saves time and allows consumers to compare prices before deciding on their purchase.

Cons of credit

The main cons of using credit are the possibility of getting into financial difficulty and not being able to make repayments. There is also the possibility of having a credit card stolen and used illegally.

Financial difficulty

People who make too many purchases may find themselves unable to make the agreed payments to the credit provider. They can then have valuable possessions, including their house, taken away from them.

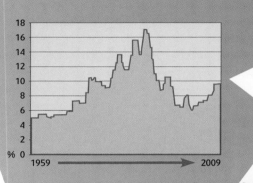

Rising rates

Interest rates do not always remain at the same level. People who use credit may find themselves having to pay back more than they expected if the interest rate rises.

Credit fraud

Some criminals are able to steal credit card details through tracking Internet use. They do not need the actual credit card to make purchases in the credit card holder's name.

3. Blanking

Large coils of metal are fed through a blanking press. This machine punches out round disks called blanks. The blanks are washed, checked for shape, and sent through another machine that creates the rims.

Making Money

Banknotes are made in a printer. They are either made from paper—usually cotton paper—or from a chemical compound called polymer. Polymer bills are stronger and harder to forge than paper bills. Coins are made in a building known as a mint. The steps for making coins are shown on these pages.

Quite a lot of thought goes into the design of money, from size and color to the images that feature on them.

1. Designing

The images on the coin often reflect an important part of a country's background, or its values. While initial design ideas may be sketched on paper, the final design is completed using computer software.

2. Making the die

A die is a cylindrical piece of metal used for making coins. Two dies are used to make each coin, and each has the design of the head or tail of the coin engraved into it.

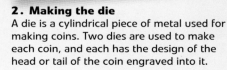

4. Pressing
Once the blanks have been created, they are placed in between the two dies. Tons of pressure are then applied to create the impression of the design on both sides of the blank.

5. Inspecting
Coins go through a machine that rejects misshapen coins, and an inspector uses a magnifying glass to check that there are no marks or other flaws on the coins.

6. Packing
Perfect coins are placed in an automatic counting machine that fills bags with a certain amount of coins. The bags are stored in secure vaults at the mint before being transported to banks.

Security features
Euro banknotes have several features
that make it hard for them to be copied.

Invisible number
When this part of the
bill is held to the light,
the value of the bill
becomes visible.

Hologram
Tilted one way, the
hologram displays the value
of the bill and the euro
symbol. Tilted the other
way, it displays the value
of the bill and a doorway
or window.

Color change
Tilting the bill causes
the numeral in the
bottom right-hand
corner of the back to
change color from
purple to green.

Fighting Fraud

Because of the financial power of money and credit cards, criminals are always trying to produce fake banknotes or illegally obtain credit card details.

Such illegal activity is not new. Changes to coins have been made for thousands of years because of attempts to produce fake coins. Changes to banknotes have been made for hundreds of years for the same reason.

That's Amazing!

The largest credit card fraud involved the theft of details of more than 130 million accounts by an American man, Albert Gonzalez. He is currently serving 20 years imprisonment.

Credit card fraud

Credit card companies fight fraud by using encryption technology. When they store their customers' credit card numbers, they encrypt it. This is similar to using a code. Anyone who gets hold of these numbers illegally will find them useless, as they will not work until they have been decrypted back into their original sequence.

SKIMMING DEVICES

Skimming is a fraud that involves using a device to copy the information kept on the magnetic strip of a credit card. Criminals secretly attach these devices to automated teller machines (ATMs). They often also place a camera nearby so they can record the customer's secret number being typed into the ATM. With this information, they are able to create fake cards and withdraw that customer's money.

Money Through the Ages

Communities have used money for thousands of years. Before there were coins and banknotes, people traded all sorts of precious commodities. No matter what was being used as currency, the idea was always the same: to use something convenient as a means of buying and selling goods.

3000–2000 BC
Inscriptions on a clay tablet from the ancient land of Mesopotamia recorded the movement of goods. This made it easy to see who was owed goods by whom.

1391–1353 BC
From the time of the eighteenth dynasty in Egypt, cattle, along with sheep, pigs, and goats, were used as a commodity to swap for other goods.

AD 880s
This is the head and tail of the silver penny from the time of King Alfred of England, who helped to strengthen the West Saxon economy through monetary reform.

1260s
During the time of Kublai Khan, the great leader of the Mongols, goods were paid for with paper money made from the bark of the mulberry tree.

FRANCE

$100 WILL BUY THIS CAR MUST HAVE CASH LOST ALL ON THE STOCK MARKET

£20

50 EURO

50 EURO

1545
King Henry VIII of England legalized the charging of interest on loans. He set an upper limit of 10 percent per year.

1694
The Bank of England was founded. The earliest seventeenth-century handwritten paper money issued by the bank is compared with today's 20-pound banknote.

1929
The Wall Street Crash in October 1929 led to the Great Depression. People were forced to sell valuable objects to pay for basic items such as food.

1957
The Treaty of Rome in 1957 led to the European Economic Community. By trading with each other, European countries gained many benefits.

1999
The euro, the European single currency, was created in 1999. It is now the sole currency in 16 countries.

Collecting Money

Some people treat money as more than just something to spend. They collect coins and bills in much the same way as some people collect stamps. People who collect coins and banknotes are called numismatists.

There are so many different coins and bills in the world that most numismatists collect coins or bills that fit into a particular theme. For example, they may collect money from a certain country or continent, banknotes of a certain color, or coins that feature similar images, such as types of transportation. Numismatists try to collect bills and coins that have never been used. The better their condition, the more valuable they are. Some coins and bills are made just for collectors and are never put into circulation.

Notaphily
The collecting of banknotes is more recent than the collecting of coins. This is mainly because coins have been around for much longer. As a result, rare banknotes do not sell for as high a price as rare coins. Banknote collecting is known as notaphily.

Kept together
Collectors keep their coins in albums. This keeps them in good condition and stops them from getting lost. Older coins are not necessarily more valuable than newer ones. The most valuable coins are those of which there are very few examples.

Damage control
A magnifying glass helps collectors determine whether there is any damage on a coin. The more damaged it is, the less valuable it becomes.

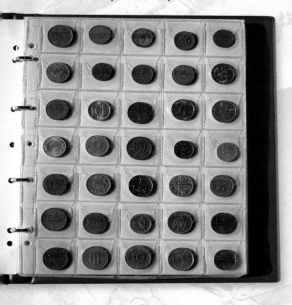

That's Amazing!

The highest recorded price ever paid for a coin is US$7,590,020. This was in 2002 for a 1933 20-dollar coin known as the Double Eagle.

Getting together

Serious numismatists get together regularly to compare and sell coins and bills from their collections. They have to stay informed on the value of their collections so they do not sell something for less than it is worth.

Glossary

barter (BAR-tur) To swap an item (or items) for another item (or items).

circulate (SER-kyuh-layt) To flow from person to person, or place to place.

colonial (kuh-LOH-nee-ul) When one country is ruled by the government of another country.

compound (KOM-pownd) Something made up of two or more chemical ingredients.

compressed (kum-PREST) Pressed together.

cons (KAHNZ) Disadvantages.

credit (KREH-dit) Borrowing money to buy something now for which you will pay later.

credit card (KREH-dit KARD) A card that enables a person to buy something using credit.

credit provider (KREH-dit pruh-VY-der) A company that lends money to people for credit purchases.

deposit (dih-PAH-zut) To put away for safekeeping.

direct debit (dih-REKT DEH-bit) When a payment is transferred from one bank account to another bank account electronically.

economic depression (eh-kuh-NAH-mik dih-PREH-shun) When a country has a lot of people out of work and people do not have much money to spend.

encryption (in-KRIP-shun) Conversion of valuable information into code to protect against theft.

flaws (FLAWZ) Mistakes.

fraud (FROD) Cheating people out of money.

hologram (HAH-luh-gram) A pattern produced by a photographic process known as holography.

ingot (ING-git) A bar of a precious metal, for example, gold.

interest (IN-ter-est) Money a person pays for borrowing money.

numismatist (noo-MIZ-muh-tist) Someone who collects coins and banknotes.

precious (PREH-shus) Valuable.

profit (PRAH-fit) Selling something for more money than it cost to produce .

pros (PROHZ) Advantages.

purchaser (PUR-chus-er) Someone who buys a product or pays for a service.

skimming (SKIM-ing) An illegal activity that involves attaching a special device to an ATM and stealing money from people's accounts.

transaction (tranz-AK-shun) The act of buying or selling something.

vault (VAWLT) A strong compartment in which precious items can be placed for safekeeping.

withdraw (with-DRAW) To take out.

Index

Websites

Due to the changing nature of Internet links, PowerKids Press has developed an online list of websites related to the subject of this book. This site is updated regularly. Please use this link to access the list: www.powerkidslinks.com/disc/money/

Westminster Public Library
3705 W. 112th Ave.
Westminster, CO 80031
www.westminsterlibrary.org